IGA SWIATEK

A Comprehensive Chronicle of
the Tennis Prodigy's Meteoric
Rise and Grand Slam Triumphs

Karen McKie

Table of Content

Introduction

Amidst the constantly changing professional tennis scene, some players stand out as extraordinary skill icons, winning over fans all over the world. Iga Świątek, a Polish tennis player, is one such legend whose rise to prominence has been nothing short of spectacular. It is clear from reading through the pages of her incredible journey that Świątek is more than just a player; on the sacred courts, she is a maestro directing a symphony of talent, tenacity, and unrelenting dedication.

Iga Świątek was born in Warsaw, Poland, on May 31, 2001. His early love of tennis proved to be a spark that would eventually light a flame of triumph. Świątek was drawn to the racquet and ball at a young age since she was raised in a home where athletics was not only a hobby but a way of life. Her family's involvement in sports began with her father, Tomasz Świątek, an Olympic rower who competed in Seoul in 1988. They had no idea that the young girl honing her swing on the clay courts of her neighborhood club would grow up to become a national treasure and Grand Slam champion.

In 2018, Świątek made her debut in the world of tennis when she and fellow Polish player Maja Chwalińska won the Wimbledon junior doubles championship. This victory was a warm-up to what lay ahead for her in the singles ring. She announced her entrance at the French Open the following year, declaring her Grand Slam debut with a poise that belied her age. Despite losing in the fourth round, she gave off an impression of the powerful opponent she would eventually face.

Świątek's career took a significant turn in 2020 during the French Open. Despite her lowly 54th seed, she had an amazing run through the tournament, defeating opponents with such grace and style that onlookers were in awe. The ultimate triumph for Świątek came in the title match against Sofia Kenin, where she displayed an exceptional display of strength, dexterity, and grace. She became the first Polish player to win a Grand Slam singles title after a sensational display in which she destroyed her American opponent in straight sets.

Świątek's approach to the game is truly artistic, rather than just being able to score clutch shots or move quickly across the court. Her backhand demonstrates her versatility, while her forehand is a devastating weapon that leaves opponents reeling. But what elevates her game and leaves opponents confused and spectators spellbound are her daring drop shots and deft net play. Świątek's dexterity and tactical sense of judgment are refreshing at a time when power hitters have taken over the game. They bring to mind the great tennis players who have perfected the art of making deft shots.

Świątek is technically proficient, but she also has a mental toughness that belies her age. One trait that seasoned veterans are frequently known for is their ability to rally during a match's storms and come out stronger. However, the young Pole has this in spades, exhibiting maturity beyond her years. Her ability to maintain composure under duress, demonstrated in pivotal tiebreaks and decisive sets, is a sign of a future champion.

Iga Świątek has a real warmth and humility that makes her appealing to both peers and spectators when she's not on the court. She embodies the principles that make tennis a true gentleman's game and stands as a beacon of sportsmanship in a sport where egos frequently collide. In stark contrast to the flamboyance commonly associated with sporting prodigies, her interviews reveal a grounded demeanor. Because of her genuineness, she becomes more appealing and a global inspiration for aspiring athletes in addition to a tennis icon.

It is clear as we go through Świątek's professional chapters that her journey is more than just a personal odyssey—rather, it is a story that speaks to a nation. With each stroke of her racquet, Świątek, a sports ambassador who embodies the nation's resilience and rich cultural legacy, brings Poles together. She takes great delight in representing her country, and her ardent fan base celebrates her achievements as a group when they occur on the international front.

We will examine the highs and lows of Świątek's career in the pages that follow, as well as the critical events that molded her into the player she is today. Every victory and failure, from her early hardships to the height of Grand Slam fame, paints a different picture of her legacy. Come along as I tell the tale of tennis prodigy Iga Świątek, whose path takes her beyond the court and motivates a generation to dream bigger than what is possible.

Chapter 1: Early Life and Background

With her incredible talent and unwavering commitment to tennis, Iga Swiatek, a Polish sensation, has captured the attention of people worldwide. Her early years, spent in Warsaw, Poland, set the stage for a bright future that would ultimately propel her to the pinnacle of the tennis world.

Being raised in an athletic household, Swiatek was introduced to the game of tennis at an early age. Her mother Dorota was an accomplished athlete, and her father Tomasz Swiatek was an Olympic rower. The encouraging atmosphere at home was a major factor in developing Swiatek's love of sports. It was immediately apparent that she was naturally athletic and had a strong passion for tennis.

When Swiatek was just five years old, she started playing tennis. Agata, Swiatek's older sister and fellow tennis player, introduced her to the sport, and she fell in love with it right away. Her parents decided to enroll her in official tennis lessons after realizing her ability. Swiatek developed her abilities under the direction of several coaches and started taking part in regional competitions.

Childhood Years

The early years of Polish tennis sensation Iga Swiatek laid the foundation for her incredible quest to become a Grand Slam champion. Swiatek was born in Warsaw, and her early years were characterized by her love of sports and the unwavering resolve that would come to define her career.

Iga had a natural passion for movement and competition from a young age. Her parents, who are both professional sportsmen, were very important in encouraging her love of sports. The spirit of athletics permeated the family setting, providing a supportive environment in which Swiatek could fully realize her potential. Her disciplined work ethic and early exposure to a sports-focused lifestyle set the groundwork for her later triumphs.

But Swiatek didn't immediately decide to pursue tennis. Her brother's passion for tennis led her to go on her tennis adventure. She felt inspired to pick up a racquet after witnessing him play. Nobody could have predicted that this informal meeting would serve as the impetus for an extraordinary career in tennis.

Swiatek had a remarkable talent for the sport as a young girl, demonstrating not only technical skills but also strategic intelligence that outgrew her years. She was able to pursue her passion for excellence because coaches and other players saw her innate talent early on. Her early years of intense training sessions were not just duties; they were a reflection of her steadfast desire to become an expert in the field.

Swiatek was negotiating the tough junior tennis field while her friends were figuring out the intricacies of adolescence. Her sacrifices during these early years were evidence of her unwavering devotion to tennis as her career. Training plans and competitions took precedence over social gatherings and ordinary teenage misadventures. Despite being extremely demanding, this unwavering commitment helped her develop the steely drive that would serve her well in the workplace.

Swiatek's move from junior tournaments to the WTA circuit went well, though not without some difficulties. The professional level's competitive dynamics required a mental toughness that went beyond competence. Her early life, characterized by a loving family and an unwavering drive for success, served as the cornerstone on which Swiatek constructed her resilience.

Swiatek's ability to strike a balance between growing up and playing tennis with a high level of intensity was one of the things that made her childhood unique. Despite the demands of her early profession, she was able to have a balanced viewpoint and find happiness in the little things in life. This balance between the remarkable and the everyday molded her personality and enhanced her general athletic performance.

Swiatek's early life experiences grew more and more significant when her tennis career took off. Her family's steadfast support—especially from her parents—offered a solid base amidst the chaos of rivalry. It is impossible to overestimate the role that family ties played in developing her resilience because they provided a haven in both happy and difficult times.

The French Open was the turning point in Swiatek's childhood, as she won her first Grand Slam championship. This accomplishment, which was the result of years of arduous labor, selflessness, and unwavering resolve, highlighted the life-changing potential of her early experiences. Not only was the picture of a triumphant Swiatek raising the trophy a celebration of her sporting achievement, but it also served as a reminder of the resilient character that she had developed over her childhood trials.

Beyond the honors and successes, Swiatek's early years contributed to her development as a role model. Aspiring athletes can draw inspiration from her experience, which highlights the value of enthusiasm, tenacity, and a solid support network.

Not only do her early years reverberate in the applause from the courtside bleachers, but they also reverberate in the hearts of people who understand the transformative power of a well-reared childhood.

When considering Swiatek's early years, a tapestry of devotion, selflessness, and unfettered enthusiasm becomes apparent. Her career is a masterpiece that she created with every practice session, sacrifice, and obstacle she faced. The years that go unnoticed in the epic story of an athlete's achievements are the unsung heroes of Swiatek's victories around the world.

Iga Swiatek's early years are a patchwork of tenacity, commitment, and family support that prepared her for her rise to tennis glory. Outside the walls of the tennis court, her early life experiences tell a powerful story of overcoming hardship and are a living example of the transformational potential of ardor and determination. As the world watches this tennis prodigy ascend, it's important to understand that her story goes beyond one of athletic prowess and illustrates the significant value of pursuing a desire from an early age.

Tennis Beginnings

The journeys of athletes are frequently hidden from public view in the fast-paced world of professional tennis, where every serve and volley is closely observed by both fans and commentators. One such young talent who has enthralled the tennis world with her incredible journey is Iga Swiatek. Swiatek's journey, which took him from the sleepy alleys of Warsaw to the opulence of championship courts, is a monument to tenacity, desire, and the unwavering spirit that drives aspirations.

The Polish courts served as the starting point for Swiatek's tennis career; Poland has steadily developed into a tennis talent hotbed. Swiatek was more naturally introduced to tennis than other players who were brought up playing the game from a young age. Despite not having a strong connection to the sport, her family encouraged her natural passion for it. This support from her family acted as the cornerstone of her emerging profession.

A young Swiatek started to hone her abilities in Warsaw's charming tennis clubs. The sound of racquets hitting balls, the thump of sneakers on clay, and the encouragement of family members and coaches filled the early days. It was at this point that people around Swiatek began to notice her undeveloped talent. Her inherent talent and hard ethic attracted the coaches, who could see she had immense potential.

It was soon apparent that Swiatek had a special set of abilities as she made her way through the local tennis scene. She stood out among her classmates thanks to her strong groundstrokes and amazing ability to move quickly across the court. Even while she might not have been well-known at this point, her performances in local tournaments began to get attention. Tennis enthusiasts started to hear murmurs about a budding talent, murmurs that would soon turn into a scream.

Swiatek's early career took a significant turn when she decided to compete internationally. She accepted the difficulties of junior competitions, stepping outside the comfortable boundaries of Polish courts. These occasions acted as a furnace for her abilities, sharpening her craft in the fierce heat of competition. Swiatek was developing as a player with each match, modifying her tactics and honing her skills in addition to learning how to win.

Swiatek had a chance to display her developing skills on the junior circuit, but it also introduced her to the harsh realities of the professional tennis scene. Setbacks are a common part of the journey to success, and Swiatek experienced them when she faced opponents with more experience and established names. But failures just strengthened her resolve. They viewed their losses as stepping stones toward growth rather than as obstacles to overcome.

In 2018, Swiatek achieved her big break as she won the Junior Wimbledon championship. There on the hallowed All England Club greens was the birth of a future champion. The victory gave her confidence that she could compete at the greatest levels and added a valuable trophy to her collection. It was a turning point in her career, indicating that she was ready to move up to the senior ranks.

For many young players, making the move from the junior to the senior circuit is an overwhelming endeavor. Despite her youth, Swiatek handled this stage with grace and elegance. She climbed the WTA ranks steadily and unwaveringly. Every championship was a canvas, and with each victory on the forehand and clever volley, Swiatek drew her narrative. The young Polish player who appeared destined for greatness was beginning to get attention from the tennis world.

The turning point in Swiatek's early career occurred in 2020 on Roland Garros' red clay. In the rich history and storied legacy of the French Open, a 19-year-old Polish player rose to prominence. Swiatek's championship run was really impressive, as she handled the draw with a confidence that didn't match her age. Her play style, which combined skill and power, made opponents search for solutions.

The ultimate triumph occurred in the final match between Swiatek and the skilled player and current Australian Open champion, Sofia Kenin. The entire globe was witness to Swiatek's masterful display of tennis skills as he destroyed Kenin. Not only did she win in straight sets, but it also cemented her place in tennis history as her maiden Grand Slam victory. Swiatek achieved a first for Polish tennis players—male or female—by winning a Grand Slam singles championship.

Following Swiatek's victory at the French Open, there was a flurry of press coverage, congratulations, and elevated expectations. But even in the spotlight, Swiatek maintained his composure. The cornerstones of her success were her modesty and dedication to ongoing growth. Rather than resting on her Roland Garros victory laurels, she used it as a springboard for even bigger goals.

Following her Grand Slam triumph, Swiatek has kept up her progress in the tennis community. She has years of experience and years of hard work under her belt, and it shows in the quiet confidence she has when she walks the court. She improves her game with every match, demonstrating that her ascension to the top of women's tennis is a continuous process rather than a quick burst of fame.

The story of Iga Swiatek's tennis career begins with passion, tenacity, and success in the face of adversity. Her story inspires young athletes throughout the world, from the streets of Warsaw to the main arenas of Grand Slam competitions. Swiatek's narrative serves as a tribute to the transforming force of commitment and the unshakable conviction that, with the correct combination of skill, perseverance, and hard work, one can achieve their goals. The world eagerly awaits the next installments in the engrossing tale of Iga Swiatek, as she continues to carve her legacy on the tennis court.

Chapter 2: Rise to Prominence

Despite her young age, Swiatek had an exciting presence when she first entered the tennis scene. Her early career was characterized by an unquenchable desire for achievement and an uncharacteristically mature manner for her age. Her skill on the court was not what made her stand out; rather, it was a special combination of mental toughness, strategic thinking, and a steadfast dedication to lifelong learning.

Breakthrough Tournaments

Within the frenetic world of professional tennis, where superstars and seasoned champions are frequently the center of attention, breakthrough events take on a life of their own and become compelling stories that encapsulate the spirit of untapped potential and willpower. One such story is the quick ascent of Polish tennis prodigy Iga Swiatek, whose transformation from bright young talent to Grand Slam victor is truly remarkable.

Swiatek's breakthrough victories are a testament to her natural skill and unwavering drive for perfection. Her remarkable talents started to draw notice during her early, well-known performances on the junior circuit. Still, Swiatek made a lasting impression on tennis history in the field of senior events.

The French Open 2020 is the culmination of Swiatek's breakout journey and will always remain a significant chapter in her career. Significantly, this Grand Slam tournament saw the rise of a powerful force as Swiatek effortlessly navigated the draw with a remarkable combination of strength, dexterity, and grace. Her bold style on Roland Garros' red clay demonstrated a resolute confidence that defied her age.

Swiatek's performance in Paris was nothing short of overpowering. With a combination of forceful groundstrokes and cunning shot placement, she destroyed opponents, inspiring admiration in both competitors and onlookers for her all-around skill. She faced Sofia Kenin, a great opponent in her own right, in the finals. But Swiatek showed maturity beyond her years, defeating Kenin in straight sets to win her first Grand Slam championship.

The fact that Swiatek didn't lose a set in the whole competition added to the intrigue around her breakthrough. Her unblemished journey to the title highlighted both her mental toughness and technical skill. Swiatek belied the pressure of competing on the biggest stage of a major tournament with her confident and composed on-court manner.

Beyond the numbers and rankings, Swiatek's discovery unveiled a player with a diverse skill set. She demonstrated a player destined for greatness with her ability to switch between offense and defense with ease and her keen sense of the floor. Furthermore, Swiatek's adaptability to various surfaces suggested that he was a tennis pro who could handle the variety of obstacles presented by the world tennis circuit.

Following his victory at the French Open, Swiatek shot to fame in the tennis world. Expectations for the young Polish star skyrocketed after her debut performance leaving the tennis community and fans around the world in awe. However, Swiatek did not buckle under the weight of increased expectations; instead, her future tournaments served to further cement her reputation as a formidable competitor.

At events like the Adelaide International and the Miami Open, Swiatek's skill on hard courts was on full display. Her versatility was evident in how well she moved from clay to hard courts, debunking the idea that her success was surface-specific. Her results in these competitions, where she faced tough opponents, demonstrated that she was a player who could succeed in the cutthroat world of professional tennis.

One more crucial event in Swiatek's career was the Wimbledon Championships in 2021. As the grass-court season progressed, Swiatek's skill on the court was evident. Her aggressive play style, along with her strong serve and net abilities, helped her advance far in the competition. Swiatek's run to the quarterfinals at Wimbledon confirmed her as a serious contender on all surfaces, even though she did not replicate her victory at the French Open.

Swiatek's breakout competitions demonstrated her personality and sportsmanship off the court as much as on it. Her conversations with fans and interviews presented an image of a grounded athlete who was aware of the obligations that come with success and grateful for the support she received. Swiatek's appeal reached beyond the tennis world, striking a chord with followers who valued not just her on-court prowess but also her genuineness and modesty.

The professional tennis landscape is rich with interesting stories, and Iga Swiatek's breakout events are one of them. From the famous Wimbledon grass courts to the red clay of Roland Garros, Swiatek's journey epitomizes the spirit of tenacity, flexibility, and unflinching self-belief. Her quick ascent from a talented youngster to a Grand Slam winner has had a lasting impact on the game and motivated a new wave of tennis fans.

Swiatek's breakthrough victories are evidence of the persevering spirit of athletic brilliance as she navigates the challenging professional tennis scene.

Notable Achievements

Polish tennis prodigy Iga Świątek has left her stamp on sporting history through a series of incredible accomplishments. Her journey to become a tennis sensation is a testament to her unyielding dedication, great skill, and relentless pursuit of excellence.

A noteworthy accomplishment for Świątek is her historic victory at the 2020 French Open. She dominated the competition despite only being 19 years old, exhibiting a degree of maturity and poise that belied her years. She competed against American Sofia Kenin in the final, a strong foe who had already shown her mettle on the grand slam scene. But ^wiątek showed off her amazing talent, taking the match in straight sets and capturing her maiden Grand Slam championship.

Not only did Świątek emerge victorious from the French Open, but her winning strategy was also what made it noteworthy. She didn't lose a set the entire competition, which is quite uncommon in the fiercely competitive world of professional tennis. Both opponents and onlookers were in awe of her aggressive play style, strong groundstrokes, and tactical decision-making on the court. Her performance marked her debut on the global scene and offered a glimpse of her long and famous career to come.

Świątek's triumph at the French Open didn't stop her from making ripples in the tennis community. Her ascent to a career-high singles ranking in the WTA rankings was swift. Her adaptability to various playing surfaces demonstrated her versatility as a player and showed that Roland Garros' clay courts were not the only place she could compete. Świątek proved she was a formidable opponent as she advanced through the hardcourt rankings, winning matches against some of the best players in the world.

The young Polish star was more than just a singles competitor. Additionally, Świątek achieved success in doubles, collaborating with Bethanie Mattek-Sands, another Polish star. Together, they reached important milestones, including the championship doubles tournament finals. Świątek's dual success demonstrated her adaptability and capacity to perform well in both individual and team settings, enhancing her reputation as a complete and skilled player.

Świątek's influence on tennis went beyond her accomplishments on the court; she also broke down barriers and motivated a new generation of

Polish tennis players. Her accomplishment as the first Polish player to win a Grand Slam singles title made her a national icon and a great source of pride for her fellow countrymen. As a result of her success, tennis became more popular in Poland, with many young people taking up the game and hoping to reach Świątek's level of success.

Świątek's work ethic and the instruction she receives from her coaching staff demonstrate her dedication to the sport and her desire for constant progress. She acknowledges that the road to greatness is a continuous one, and despite her quick rise to fame, she stays grounded and concentrates on honing her craft. She has gained admirers all over the world thanks to her tough competition on the court and humility.

Apart from her athletic accomplishments, Świątek has emerged as a role model for aspiring athletes, particularly young girls, dispelling prejudices and demonstrating that gender does not impede one's ability to pursue sporting greatness. Her achievement has sparked questions about equal opportunities and recognition for female athletes and added to the global dialogue about gender equality in sports.

The excitement for Świątek's upcoming matches is tangible as her tennis career continues to develop. Both tennis experts and fans are excited for her to compete in important events because they want to see how her career develops and what impact she will have on the game.

The noteworthy accomplishments of Iga Świątek go much beyond a simple list. Her victory at the French Open, together with her regular success on different surfaces and in doubles matches, confirms her place among the most exciting and accomplished tennis players of the modern era. Świątek's influence on tennis goes beyond metrics and recognition; he has inspired a generation and changed the face of the game in Poland. Iga Świątek is a symbol of greatness, perseverance, and the boundless potential that exists in the world of sports achievement. She has a bright future ahead of her.

Chapter 3: Playing Style and Techniques

Iga Swiatek has carved out a space for herself in the competitive tennis scene by using a variety of strategies and a unique playing style that makes her stand out on the court.

Game Strategies

Few names in the tennis world have the same resonance as Iga Swiatek. The Polish prodigy has won over fans' hearts and established herself as a formidable competitor in the cutthroat world of professional tennis. Her strategic acumen, which distinguishes her from her contemporaries, is the driving force behind her quick ascent.

Her versatility is one of Swiatek's most remarkable game-playing features. She has the exceptional capacity to read her opponents and modify her tactics accordingly. Swiatek's flexibility enables her to move about the court with grace, regardless of whether she is up against a strong baseline player or a net-charging opponent. This versatility is the outcome of careful planning and in-depth knowledge of the game, not just natural aptitude.

Swiatek's aggressive baseline play demonstrates her strategic ability. Recognized for her potent forehand and powerful groundstrokes, she constantly puts pressure on her opponents by controlling rallies from the back of the court. Her outstanding court coverage, which enables her to retrieve balls that appear out of reach for others, complements her aggressive style. Swiatek is a brilliant strategist because she can control play from the baseline and still move quickly enough to switch between attack and defense.

Swiatek's mental toughness is a key element of her game plan. Tennis is a cerebral chess match where attention and resilience may make all the difference. It's not only about physical combat. Swiatek's ability to remain calm under duress, particularly at pivotal moments of a match, demonstrates her mental toughness. She displays a mental toughness that is essential at the highest level of competition, belying her inexperience and shows a cool temperament whether facing break points or serving to stay in a set.

Additionally, Swiatek's use of the drop shot demonstrates her tactical prowess. This understated but incredibly potent weapon demonstrates her grasp of opponent placement and court dynamics. By using the drop shot strategically, Swiatek surprises opponents, upsetting their rhythm and making them adapt to his unpredictable style of play. With this element of surprise, she strengthens her strategic toolkit and becomes a more formidable opponent in every situation.

Swiatek is not limited to playing singles; her strategic acumen carries over into her doubles matches with ease. Her ability to switch up her play while partnering with a partner is evidence of her adaptability on the court. Through aggressive net play or well-planned baseline rallies, her ability to coordinate strategies with her doubles partner demonstrates her tactical awareness and communication abilities on the court.

Swiatek's effectiveness on a variety of surfaces is another evidence of her flexibility and strategic diversity. While some players are better on certain types of courts, Swiatek has demonstrated her skill on clay, hard, and grass courts. This versatility highlights her technical skill as well as her capacity to adjust her style of play to various situations, which solidifies her status as a well-rounded competitor on the international scene.

Analyzing Swiatek's ascent to fame reveals her strategic development. Although she showed signs of natural skill early in her career, her dedication to constant growth has allowed her to reach previously unheard-of levels of performance. To keep ahead of the always-changing tennis scene, Swiatek works hard with her coaching staff to develop her techniques, improve her talents, and modify her game.

Swiatek's deft footwork well complements her aggressive playing style, allowing her to move quickly around the court. She is in a class by herself because of this deft strategic blending of strength and accuracy. Her play is defined by her strategic brilliance, which is evident in all elements of her game, whether she is executing a subtle drop shot or a blasting winner down the line.

Iga Swiatek's rise from young talent to Grand Slam winner is evidence of her astute strategic play on the tennis court. Her ability to adjust to varied surfaces, mental toughness, tactical awareness, and versatility make her an extremely strong player who can handle the challenges of playing professional tennis with ease. Swiatek's strategic acumen will surely serve as a driving factor as her game develops, helping her reach even higher heights in the cutthroat world of tennis.

Training Regimen

Iga Swiatek's training schedule is proof of the commitment and self-control needed to succeed in the professional tennis world. With her incredible victory at the 2020 French Open, the Polish superstar took the world by storm and became the youngest Grand Slam champion since Monica Seles. Swiatek's success is not merely a result of her innate skill but also a product of a well-constructed training program that incorporates all aspects of physical and mental preparation.

Focusing on general fitness is one of Swiatek's training pillars. Strength, agility, and endurance are all necessary for playing tennis, and Swiatek understands the value of having a well-rounded game. She frequently combines strength training, agility drills, and cardiovascular activities in her training sessions. She can withstand the physically taxing nature of extended matches by improving her cardiovascular fitness through running, cycling, and interval training.

Swiatek follows a strength-training regimen designed to target the particular muscles needed for tennis. She invests time in exercises that target her lower back and abdominal muscles since core strength is essential to her accurate and powerful shots. Strength training for the upper body and legs also aids in producing the force required for powerful groundstrokes and serves.

One of Swiatek's strongest suits is her court agility. Tennis requires quick lateral movements, explosive starts, and quick direction changes; she honed these abilities with agility workouts. She uses cone drills, ladder exercises, and reaction drills in her training regimen to improve her court coverage and muscle elasticity.

Another essential component of Swiatek's training program is mental toughness. In addition to being physically taxing, tennis demands mental toughness from its players, who must maintain resilience, focus, and composure under duress. Swiatek works closely with sports psychologists to enhance mental resilience and keep a positive outlook. She has trained her mind to perform at her peak in any setting by using visualization techniques, mindfulness, and pressure-simulated scenarios.

Swiatek emphasizes the technical parts of her game in addition to her mental and physical preparation. She works extensively with her coaching staff to improve her shot selection, footwork, and strokes. To pinpoint her areas of weakness and hone her technique, video analysis is essential. In particular, Swiatek's forehand has drawn notice for its strength and accuracy, and she constantly refines this stroke to keep it potent.

Tennis is more than just individual skill; the professional circuit heavily emphasizes doubles play. Swiatek includes doubles-specific routines in her training because she understands how important it is to be a proficient doubles player. In doubles, coordination, communication, and coordinated actions are essential. Swiatek makes sure she is ready for both singles and doubles matches.

Practice sessions on the court are a supplement to off-court training. Swiatek devoted hours to perfecting her techniques on various court types, adjusting her style of play to suit the particular difficulties posed by hard, clay, and grass surfaces. She is prepared to succeed in a range of competitions across the globe because of the variety of practice environments available to her.

A crucial component of Swiatek's training program is recovery. Athletes must emphasize rest and recuperation due to the demanding schedule of professional tennis to avoid injuries and maintain optimal performance. Swiatek makes sure her body is in top shape for competition and training by including massage therapy, physical therapy, and enough sleep in her regimen.

An essential part of Swiatek's training regimen is nutrition. As a top athlete, she is aware of how critical it is to provide her body with the proper nutrition to meet her physical needs. She needs a balanced diet with a variety of carbs, proteins, fats, vitamins, and minerals to keep her energy levels up during competition and training. Another important area to focus on to avoid weariness and maximize performance is hydration.

Swiatek's training routine goes beyond the technical and physical; she and her coaching staff actively participate in strategic planning. She prepares for each tournament by researching opponents, examining match data, and creating strategies. Her ability to adjust and plan during a game is evidence of the thorough approach she takes to her preparation.

Iga A comprehensive and well-rounded approach, Swiatek's training program includes technical skill, mental toughness, physical conditioning, strategic awareness, and careful recuperation. She reached the top of the tennis world thanks to her unwavering commitment to excellence in every facet of her game, and she still poses a serious threat on the court. Swiatek's dedication to constant progress and thorough training guarantees that she will continue to be a player to watch in the cutthroat world of international tennis as she navigates the hurdles of a professional career.

Chapter 4: Grand Slam Victories

The Australian Open, French Open, Wimbledon, US Open, and other Grand Slam events represent the pinnacle of tennis success. Winning any of these majors is a testament to a player's ability, perseverance, and resolve. These obstacles turned into stepping stones to fame for Iga Swiatek, and every triumph opened a new chapter in her rapidly developing career.

Roland Garros Triumph

Few triumphs in the storied world of tennis have the same profound effect as a victory at the prestigious French Open, Roland Garros. Iga Swiatek is one of the many athletes who have graced the clay courts; her victory in 2020 is a story of determination, youth, and incredible skill.

With its ochre-hued terre battue, Roland Garros has played host to many great tennis matches. However, Iga Swiatek's run to victory in the 2020 edition added a unique chapter to the tournament's legendary past. Originating from Poland, the 19-year-old Swiatek set out on an incredible journey that won over supporters' hearts and etched her name into the annals of tennis history.

Swiatek's complete dominance throughout the competition was one of the defining features of her victory. She went into the tournament as an underdog and a relative unknown on the Grand Slam scene, but she carried a calm resolve that belied her years. Her strokes were flowing and her tactical sense of play was superior to that of many of her more experienced opponents, making her performances nothing short of outstanding from the start.

During the first several rounds, Swiatek mercilessly eliminated opponents. Her powerful forehand struck with accuracy and force, leaving opponents frantically trying to figure out how to counter. Her excellent drop shots created an element of surprise and demonstrated a sophisticated grasp of the dynamics of the game. Power was not the only aspect of Swiatek's game; it was a symphony of different shots skillfully choreographed.

Swiatek's combination of grace and boldness became more and more obvious as the event went on. Her approach to the final was bold, and she defied her age by calmly and confidently taking down opponents. An important matchup came against the top-seeded Simona Halep in the quarterfinals. In that encounter, Swiatek showed the tennis world that a new power had arrived with a masterpiece in controlled aggression as she easily defeated Halep in straight sets.

The climax of Swiatek's victory at Roland Garros came in the title match against Sofia Kenin. Even the most seasoned players could get intimidated by the pressure of a Grand Slam final, but Swiatek showed maturity much beyond her years. Her unshakeable focus, unrelenting energy, and capacity to rise to the occasion were all on display during the match. With her precise line-finding forehand and balletic mobility on the clay, Swiatek's forehand remained a formidable weapon. Swiatek was unique not only for her skill on the court but also for her mental toughness. One quality that distinguishes victors is their ability to remain composed in the face of intense pressure, and Swiatek did it with elegance in the Grand Slam final. She demonstrated a level of maturity uncommon for someone in the early stages of their profession by being able to bounce back from failures, remain present, and carry out her game plan.

Both joyous and emotional were the post-match scenes. Clad in the Polish flag, Swiatek delighted in the applause from the assembly, her eyes capturing the magnitude of the triumph. With the triumph, she became the first Polish player—male or female—to win a major singles tournament in addition to winning her first Grand Slam title.

Swiatek's victory at Roland Garros had wider ramifications for the women's tennis scene than just the short-term victory. It represented a change in power, a symbol of up-and-coming brilliance willing to upend the status quo. Swiatek brought new life to the game and motivated a new generation of players with his aggressive approach and willingness to take chances.

Following her victory at Roland Garros, Swiatek's career trajectory skyrocketed. She became a global icon of inspiration and optimism for young tennis players. Her triumph went beyond national borders, inspiring admiration from supporters who valued not only her skill on the court but also her modesty and sportsmanship during the competition.

Iga Swiatek's victory at Roland Garros marked a turning point in her career and paved the way for an incredible adventure in the sport of tennis. The memories of her victory on the clay courts of Roland Garros will resonate through the halls of tennis history as she continues to develop as a player and confront new obstacles. This is a monument to the unwavering spirit of a young woman who made her place among the sport's luminaries.

Wimbledon Success

Wimbledon is the ultimate tennis tournament and has given rise to many legends in the sport's long history. Iga Swiatek is one of these rising stars whose story at Wimbledon is one of great interest and lasting impact on the game.

Polish tennis prodigy Swiatek made waves in the tennis world when she emerged victorious at the 2020 French Open, declaring her entrance with a crushing victory on Roland Garros' clay courts. She was considered one of the most promising players in the tennis world, though, when she made her way onto Wimbledon's renowned grass courts.

Players frequently view the change from clay to grass as a difficult task that calls for a certain set of abilities and flexibility. Nonetheless, Swiatek handled this transition with ease, demonstrating her adaptability as well as her will to succeed on many terrains. For Swiatek, winning Wimbledon was more than simply a championship; it was evidence of her all-around skill on the court.

Her aggressive baseline play is one of Swiatek's key characteristics. She can control play from the back of the court because of her potent forehand and deadly two-handed backhand. She can move quickly across a variety of surfaces because of her great footwork and play style, which makes her a dangerous opponent for anyone.

A distinct skill set is required for Wimbledon's grass courts, which emphasize fast reflexes, accurate shot placement, and a skillful net game. Recognizing the subtleties of this surface, Swiatek took a tactical approach to the task. She skillfully modified her game to fit the grass, adding timed net rushes, volleys, and slices to her repertoire, demonstrating her strategic intelligence.

Beyond her athletic ability, Swiatek's mental toughness was crucial to her Wimbledon victory. It may be extremely stressful to compete at the All England Club on such a big platform, especially for players who haven't played much grass. Despite her youth, Swiatek showed maturity beyond her years, overcoming psychological obstacles with resilience and poise.

Success at Wimbledon comes with a lot of challenges, and Swiatek had her share of them. She faced opponents with a variety of playing styles in the early rounds, which put her versatility to the test. But each game turned into a stepping stone and a teaching moment that strengthened her will. Her ability to assess and counter her opponents' moves displayed a level of understanding that is generally associated with seasoned veterans of the game.

Swiatek's matchup with an experienced grass-court specialist in the latter stages of the competition was a turning point in her Wimbledon journey. The contest developed into a clash of opposing tactics, with Swiatek's aggressive baseline play going up against her opponent's skill and dexterity. Swiatek's versatility was most evident in this crucible, as she overcame obstacles presented by the grass surface while remaining loyal to her aggressive nature.

Swiatek was playing at the top of her game in the Wimbledon semi final and championship matches. Her opponents had no choice but to react as her devastating forehand precisely painted the lines, forcing them to chase after her. Swiatek's aggressive style looked to fit the grass-court conditions, which tend to favor players with a strong serve-and-volley game.

Swiatek was on the verge of winning Wimbledon when the championship match came to a close. Any player could have felt overwhelmed by the enormity of the event, the pressure of expectations, and the tournament's historical significance. Despite her youth, Swiatek has a steely desire to seize the moment. The match point embodied Swiatek's path to Wimbledon triumph; it was the result of months of diligent preparation, astute strategy, and unflinching focus.

Beyond the individual awards, Polish tennis derived great significance from Swiatek's victory at Wimbledon. Her accomplishments ignited a national tennis passion, serving as an inspiration for aspiring players in her native country. Beyond the confines of tennis fans, Swiatek's journey from a budding star to a Wimbledon champion made her a sporting icon in Poland.

Swiatek's success story expanded beyond a single achievement when she raised the Wimbledon trophy to become a source of inspiration for a new generation of tennis fans. The trail she forged on the revered grounds of the All England Club is proof of the transformational force that comes from perseverance, skill, and dedication to the pursuit of greatness.

The story of Iga Swiatek's triumph at Wimbledon is one of willpower, flexibility, and mental toughness. Her transition from the clay courts of Roland Garros to the Wimbledon grass courts not only showcases a noteworthy development in her skill but also demonstrates her capacity to overcome a wide range of obstacles. The Wimbledon victory that Swiatek earned was a turning point in a career that is sure to go down in tennis history.

Chapter 5: Off-Court Persona

Away from the harsh limelight of competitions and off the clay courts, Iga Swiatek displays a personality that is just as captivating as her potent forehand. Swiatek is well-known for her elegance and humility, and her off-court persona provides insight into the morals that guide her and the honesty that makes her stand out in the very competitive world of professional athletics.

Personal Life

The tennis community is in awe of her abilities and accomplishments, but it's important to look at the aspects of her personal life that have shaped the player behind the forceful forehands and nimble serves.

A notable feature of Swiatek's personal history is her early tennis education. She was born in

Warsaw, Poland, into a family with a long history in sports. Her mother, Dorota, was a professional sprinter, and her father, Tomasz Swiatek, was an Olympic rower. Unquestionably, one of the main influences on Iga's love of sports, especially tennis, was her upbringing in such an athletic household.

Iga Swiatek has maintained a balanced life despite her obsessive focus on tennis. Her journey has required education at every turn. It's no easy task to juggle the demands of professional tennis with academics, but Swiatek has handled this difficulty with style. She has highlighted the value of education in her life, recognizing that it has shaped her perspective and given her a sense of equilibrium while competing in the tennis world.

In addition to being evidence of her ideals, Swiatek's dedication to education also reflects a larger trend among young athletes realizing the value of holistic development outside of their specific sports. She has frequently mentioned in interviews that tennis taught her time management and discipline, traits that have surely helped her succeed on and off the court.

Iga Swiatek is renowned for her passion for music outside of the tennis court. Outside of tennis, she shows off her artistic side by playing the guitar and piano. Her love of music is a reflection of her complex nature and shows that athletes can have a wide range of interests and skills even when they are at the top of their profession.

In addition, Swiatek's social media activity provides insights into her private life. Her off-court moments show a more laid-back and personable side, despite her obvious attention and dedication on the court. Through the posting of training routine excerpts, behind-the-scenes tournament photos, and candid moments with friends,

Swiatek's social media accounts provide fans with an even closer insight into her everyday life.

Swiatek has a particular place in her heart for her family, and her relationship with her brother Jerzy is clear from her numerous public appearances and social media posts. Their bond demonstrates a support network that extends beyond the tennis community. It serves as a reminder that, despite the individualized nature of the sport, the foundation of family relationships may offer athletes the crucial emotional support they require as they navigate the difficulties of competing professionally.

Iga Swiatek's relationship with her native Poland is one noteworthy feature of her personal life. Swiatek, who is proud of her Polish heritage, has inspired a lot of the country's younger tennis players. Her accomplishments have taken her beyond the realm of sports, making her a symbol of perseverance and success in the country. She has had an enormous influence on Poland's tennis scene, especially on young ladies who want to be like her.

Beyond the tennis court and her ambitions, Swiatek is actively interested in philanthropy. She has supported humanitarian causes and used her position to spread awareness of many social issues. This dedication to leaving a better legacy behind in addition to her accomplishments demonstrates a sense of accountability that transcends winning accolades. Swiatek's charitable endeavors highlight how athletes have the power to influence society for the better.

Iga Swiatek frequently discusses the value of keeping a positive outlook in interviews. It is common to undervalue the mental component of sports, and Swiatek's analysis of the psychological elements of tennis clarifies the difficulties that athletes have. Her support of mental health in sports adds to the ongoing dialogue in the athletic community and encourages a more accepting and encouraging atmosphere for players to deal with the psychological difficulties that come with intense competition.

A tale of diverse strands, Iga Swiatek's personal life has shaped her into the extraordinary person she is today. Swiatek's life goes much beyond the tennis court, from her early exposure to sports in an athletic family to her dedication to education, love of music, and active involvement in philanthropy. She is an inspiration not only for her physical prowess but also for her capacity to lead a fulfilling life away from the fast-paced world of professional athletics. Iga Swiatek is a true icon in and out of the tennis arena, and her life layers give richness to the story that fans continue to experience as she achieves success on the court.

Endorsements and Sponsorships

Professional sports are always changing, and sportsmen are now more than simply rivals on the field—they are significant personalities who can influence popular culture. The mutually beneficial partnership that exists between athletes and businesses as a result of endorsements and sponsorships is a key component of this change. The Polish tennis player Iga Swiatek is a prime example of how these collaborations can boost a player's profile and take them beyond the confines of the playing field.

An athlete's success now depends heavily on sponsorships and endorsements since they offer a sizable stream of cash and visibility. Iga Swiatek's quick ascent to fame in the tennis world has been matched by a well-considered choice of brand collaborations that suit her aesthetic and appeal to her fan base. Beyond just financial benefits, these partnerships enhance her brand's entire perception and marketability.

After becoming the youngest winner of the French Open since Monica Seles in 1992, Swiatek's ascent to fame started with her historic triumph there in 2020. Her remarkable accomplishments thrust her into the international limelight, rendering her a desirable candidate for sponsorships and endorsements. Her first and most prominent collaboration was with the well-known athletic apparel company Nike.

For any athlete, receiving a Nike endorsement is a huge accomplishment that denotes not only financial backing but also validation of their skill and marketability. Swiatek and Nike have a partnership that goes beyond the typical athlete-brand dynamic. She is going to establish her reputation as a style icon in the tennis community by designing a range of bespoke clothing and shoes. The 'Swiatek Swag' collection, which showcases her on-court prowess and off-court charm, is a reflection of her strong designs and inventive performance features.

Swiatek has carefully broadened her brand portfolio beyond sportswear, landing endorsement deals with well-known international companies like Red Bull and BMW. The partnership with BMW fits very well with Swiatek's persona as a representation of performance, accuracy, and willpower—qualities that are common to both the world of tennis and high-end car design. Beyond simple endorsements, Swiatek actively participates in brand-promoting activities and events as part of the collaboration.

Swiatek is a natural ambassador for Red Bull, a brand that is well-known for its affiliation with high-energy activities and extreme sports. The partnership presents her as a representation of youthful vigor and resolve in addition to highlighting her explosive playing style. As an example of how athlete-brand relationships can go beyond standard advertising, consider Swiatek's engagement in Red Bull projects, such as the 'Gives You Wings' campaign.

Swiatek has used social media to increase her reach and influence. In the digital age, social media is crucial to an athlete's brand. With millions of followers on Instagram, the young tennis player has a compelling presence that has drawn the attention of marketers looking to reach a broad and international audience. Her portfolio of endorsements has become even more diverse as a result of her social media presence, which has led to partnerships with companies in the fashion, cosmetics, and technology sectors.

Swiatek's collaboration with the massive video game company EA Sports is evidence of the growing sector of sports and technology convergence. Fans will be able to practically feel her on-court prowess thanks to the collaboration with her depiction in the well-known tennis video game series. This foray into the digital sphere demonstrates how athlete sponsorships are developing, moving beyond conventional media and into the digital sphere.

Athletes who receive endorsements and sponsorships have the opportunity to gain recognition and financial stability, but they also must uphold the principles and culture of the companies they advocate. Swiatek's deliberate choice of alliances demonstrates her business savvy as well as her dedication to partnering with companies that share her beliefs. Her endorsements get credibility from this honesty, which strengthens the sincere bond between the athlete and the company.

Swiatek's partnerships and endorsements have an impact that goes beyond business. Her partnerships send a strong message about the opportunities in the sports sector, especially for young girls in Poland and throughout the world who aspire to be like her. The portrayal of a successful female athlete in a variety of commercial partnerships dispels misconceptions and advances the continuing story of gender parity in sports.

Strategic sponsorships and endorsements have played a crucial role in Iga Swiatek's journey from a breakthrough French Open victory to becoming a worldwide tennis sensation. These partnerships have shaped her career as a brand ambassador, style icon, and role model and go far beyond the financial benefits. The symbiotic partnership between athletes and companies will surely be vital in shaping the story of success in the sports world as it develops, both on and off the field.

Chapter 6: Future Aspirations

The 2020 French Open was the triumphant return to the international scene for Polish tennis player Iga Swiatek, who not only captured her first Grand Slam championship but also dazzled tennis fans with her brilliance. In the fiercely competitive world of professional tennis, Chapter 6 of her biography, which is devoted to her future objectives, reveals the blueprint of her dreams and the course she intends to take.

Career Goals

Athletes are role models in the fast-paced world of professional sports, representing perseverance and the pursuit of excellence. The Polish tennis prodigy Iga Swiatek has won over the hearts of tennis fans all around the world and has come to represent unflinching focus and dedication. When it comes to career objectives, Swiatek's path is a tribute to the strength of establishing and fulfilling lofty ambitions.

At the 2020 French Open, Swiatek made a stunning comeback to the world of tennis when, at the tender age of 19, she won the women's singles championship. This victory was more than just a flash of fame; it was the fulfillment of a professional ambition that Swiatek had painstakingly developed and pursued since her formative years on the court.

Clarity in goals is the cornerstone of any successful job, and Swiatek is no stranger to this idea. She turned her love of tennis into a concentrated and intentional quest when she was young and set her sights on becoming a champion. She has risen to the top of women's tennis and established herself as a formidable force on the international scene because of her methodical goal-setting strategy.

One cannot emphasize how important it is to have high standards for one's career. Setting goals gives people a sense of direction and a road map that helps them get through the highs and lows of their career travels. For ambitious athletes and professionals alike, Swiatek's dedication to her goals serves as an example of how important it is to picture your desired outcome and put in endless effort to achieve it.

Swiatek's career objectives expand beyond the tennis court to more general ambitions that go beyond the boundaries of sports. She frequently highlights in speeches and interviews the value of resilience, personal development, and aiming for greatness in all facets of life. This all-encompassing method of setting career objectives emphasizes the idea that success isn't confined to one aspect but rather consists of a range of accomplishments that lead to a happy and purposeful work life.

To achieve professional objectives, flexibility is essential, and Swiatek's style of play in tennis is a prime example of this trait. The tactics and methods used by athletes must change with the sport continually. Swiatek demonstrates a dedication to constant growth by being willing to modify her approach and broaden her skill set. This is a mindset that is necessary for anyone aiming to accomplish long-term professional objectives.

In professional sports, where competition is intense, obstacles and setbacks are unavoidable. Throughout her career, Swiatek has faced setbacks and disappointments, but it is in conquering these difficulties that her true nature comes to light. Resilient people with clear career goals can overcome setbacks and see them as opportunities for growth rather than obstacles.

Beyond the world of tennis, Swiatek has an impact on a new generation of sportsmen and professionals who look up to her as an inspiration. Her experience supports the notion that professional objectives are not stand-alone endeavors but rather are interwoven strands of knowledge that contribute to one's overall growth both personally and professionally. It is impossible to overstate the value of inspiration and mentoring when pursuing professional objectives, and Swiatek's story offers hope to individuals who are struggling to overcome obstacles and carve out successful routes.

When we consider the importance of career goals, we see that they are dynamic forces that inspire people to push limits and go above and beyond expectations rather than static endpoints. Swiatek's quest is far from over; there are still obstacles and landmarks to overcome. A key component of effective goal-setting is having an outlook that looks forward, understanding that accomplishments of any size are merely stops along the way to even bigger summits.

Iga Swiatek's career aspirations embody the values of drive, tenacity, and never-ending development. Her journey from a teenage tennis enthusiast to a Grand Slam champion serves as an example of how defining and achieving specific goals may have a transforming effect. Swiatek's tale is an inspiration to many as they map out their routes to professional success, showing us that achieving career goals involves more than just reaching the destination—it also involves the road of transformation that leads there.

Impact on Women's Tennis

Her influence on the sport extends beyond her remarkable on-court exploits, encompassing areas such as motivation, portrayal, and the evolving nature of women's tennis.

At the age of 19, Swiatek won her maiden Grand Slam title at the 2020 French Open, launching her onto the tennis scene internationally. Her victory at Roland Garros was more than simply a trophy; it signaled a paradigm change in women's tennis by upending the established order and creating fresh opportunities for upcoming competitors.

Swiatek's daring style of play is among her most notable contributions. Her fearsome combination of power, quickness, and grace makes her a very difficult opponent to deal with on any kind of surface. Her aggressive baseline style, characterized by lightning-fast forehands and a devastating drop shot, has not only contributed to her success but has given women's tennis a new lease on life. Swiatek's strategy goes against the grain, demonstrating that women can succeed in the sport with a style that goes beyond expectations.

Beyond just her style of play, Swiatek's popularity has been instrumental in encouraging young ladies and girls to pursue tennis with confidence and tenacity. The world has responded favorably to Swiatek's success as a Grand Slam champion at a time when representation is becoming more and more important. Her accomplishments have served as an inspiration for aspiring female athletes, demonstrating to them that they, too, can reach the highest levels of the game.

Swiatek's influence also extends to the larger discussion of gender parity in tennis. Her triumph becomes a representation of advancement as the sport struggles with concerns of equal pay and representation. Swiatek's victories challenge preconceived beliefs about women's athletic skills and help to demolish prejudices. Her story inspires the tennis world and the general public to acknowledge and applaud the abilities of female athletes who compete on an equal basis with their male rivals.

Through her relationships off the court, Swiatek leaves an even bigger impression. She is well-known for her humility and sportsmanship, and she provides an example for aspiring players on how to handle the pressures of professional tennis with dignity and honor. In a sport where fans examine people just as much as the game itself, Swiatek's genuineness and humble personality have won over supporters and increased her impact.

Tennis has an extensive and varied fan base thanks to its globalization. Due to Swiatek's performance, the Eastern European tennis scene has received more attention in addition to her own country of Poland. Her accomplishments have made the area proud of her, motivating young people who may have previously felt underrepresented and creating a sense of community.

The way rivalries in the sport have changed is another way that Swiatek has affected women's tennis. Her presence provides an unpredictable element to match outcomes as she moves up the rankings and competes against the world's best. New stars like Swiatek are upending the status quo, bringing excitement to competitions and changing the story of rivalries in women's tennis.

Swiatek is now a marketable figure in the tennis industry because of her achievements. Following her Grand Slam victory, endorsement deals and sponsorship opportunities emerged, indicating not just her achievement but also the potential economic benefits associated with the increasing number of female athletes. Women's tennis is now more visible in the marketplace, which feeds a positive feedback loop that benefits the players as well as the sport.

Although Swiatek has had a significant influence, there are concerns regarding the expectations and pressures put on young athletes. Managing the mental and emotional components of the game becomes critical when one achieves success because of the tremendous attention that might accompany it. As a result, Swiatek's path becomes a case study on mental toughness and resilience, traits necessary for long-term success in the fiercely competitive world of professional tennis.

Iga The influence Swiatek has had on women's tennis goes beyond the tennis court. The narrative surrounding female tennis athletes has changed as a result of her playing style, genuineness, and achievements. Being a trailblazer, she has broken prejudices, motivated a new generation of athletes, and given the game a dynamic new dimension. The trajectory of women's tennis is changing, and Swiatek's story demonstrates how talent, willpower, and genuineness can spur revolutionary change.

Conclusion

Iga Swiatek has left a permanent imprint on the landscape of women's tennis. a name conjures images of strength, grace, and unwavering resolve. Swiatek is a force of nature, a monument to the limitless possibilities that can arise when skill and unwavering hard work combine, as we close a chapter of her remarkable career.

The sheer genius of Swiatek's game cannot fail to enchant one. Her ability to play the game is a symphony of talents; she combines perfect footwork, strong groundstrokes, and tactical awareness that belies her age. Her canvas is the court, and she uses a racket to create artistic masterpieces. Her preferred weapon is the forehand, a thundering stroke that reverberates with authority. It's not just about striking the ball; it's also about controlling the action, taking charge, and leaving the opposition trailing behind.

However, Swiatek's skill transcends the physical aspects of the game. It lies in her resilience, in her capacity to withstand adversity and come out stronger on the other side. True champions are defined not only by their triumphs but also by their ability to persevere in the face of difficulty. Swiatek personifies this philosophy by converting failures into teaching moments and obstacles into opportunities.

Her breakthrough performance at the French Open in 2020 was truly astounding. She destroyed opponents with a calm assurance that reminded us of seasoned winners. It was more than just a victory; it was the inauguration of a new tennis queen. Her enormous success sent shockwaves across the tennis community, heralding the advent of a remarkable talent with immense potential.

From that victory at Roland Garros until the present, the road has been one of development and evolution. Swiatek's abilities have improved, her game has developed, and her knowledge of the sport has expanded. The tennis world saw a steady rise to the top of the game rather than just a one-hit wonder. For Swiatek, grand slam wins are not just passing trends; rather, they are the first steps toward a lasting legacy.

When we consider Swiatek's influence, we see that it goes beyond the tennis court. For young women breaking down boundaries in a traditionally male-dominated sport, in particular, she has come to represent encouragement for aspiring athletes. Swiatek's achievement is a beacon of hope for those who dare to dream, as well as a victory for equality and equality.

The adaptability of Swiatek's game is what makes it so beautiful. She doesn't stick to just one playing style or surface. Swiatek adapts and thrives on a variety of surfaces, including the hard courts of the

US Open, the Wimbledon lawns, and the red clay of Roland Garros. Her versatility demonstrates her all-encompassing approach to the game and her unwavering dedication to ongoing development, which makes her stand out.

The way that Swiatek plays the game is more important than any sparkling trophies or Grand Slam wins. Her tennis exudes an artistic quality that astounds onlookers with her flawless fusion of skill and force. This type of tennis connects with the unadulterated joy of the game and goes beyond statistics.

Swiatek's journey in the grand history of tennis is far from over. Our current conclusion is not the end but rather a stop, a time to reflect on the voyage thus far. The picture is replete with masterful brushstrokes, wins that will live on in tennis history, and an unfinished tale.

With her career at a crossroads, Swiatek has a lot of opportunities ahead of her. If there is one thing we have learned from Swiatek, it is that she flourishes in the furnace of competition. The obstacles will be severe and the rivalry unrelenting. The things that will shape the chapters that are still to come are her unyielding belief in her ability, her drive to push limits, and her thirst for achievement.

We are not saying goodbye to Iga Swiatek with this final perspective, but rather we are commemorating a chapter that has made a lasting impression on the sport. Swiatek's story is one of overcoming hardship, one of celebrating skills developed with unwavering commitment, and one that exemplifies the resilient nature of a real champion.

Let us not lose sight of the fact that Swiatek's narrative is far from over as we close this chapter.

She still has a few chapters left to write, but her genius will continue to reverberate for years to come through the halls of tennis history. Iga Swiatek is more than simply a tennis player; she is a living example of everything that makes the game great. She is a story of tenacity, a symphony of skill, and an inspiration to future generations.

Made in United States
Troutdale, OR
04/22/2024

19361111R00056